THE HUMAN MACHINE

THE SKELETON AND MUSCLES

Louise Spilsbury

www.heinemann.co.uk/library
Visit our website to find out more information about Heinemann Library books.

To order:
☎ Phone 44 (0)1865 888066
▤ Send a fax to 44 (0)1865 314091
🖥 Visit the Heinemann Bookshop at www.heinemann.co.uk/library to browse our catalogue and order online.

First published in Great Britain by Heinemann, Halley Court, Jordan Hill, Oxford, OX2 8EJ, part of Harcourt Education.
Heinemann is a registered trademark of Harcourt Education Ltd.

Editorial: Nancy Dickmann and Rachel Howells
Design: Victoria Bevan and AMR Design Ltd
Illustrations: Medi-mation
Picture Research: Hannah Taylor
Production: Vicki Fitzgerald

Originated by Chroma
Printed and bound in China by CTPS

ISBN 978 0 431 19207 9 (hardback)
12 11 10 09 08
10 9 8 7 6 5 4 3 2 1

British Library Cataloguing in Publication Data
Spilsbury, Louise
Skeleton and muscles. - (The human machine)
1. Musculoskeletal system - Juvenile literature
I. Title
612.7
A full catalogue record for this book is available from the British Library.

Acknowledgements
The publishers would like to thank the following for permission to reproduce photographs: ©Alamy p. **22** (Eric Nathan); ©Corbis pp. **26** (Royalty Free), **24** (Brooke Fasani), **27** (Duomo), **10** (Image100/ Russell Glenister), **9** (Kevin Dodge), **13** (Patrik Giardino), **5** (Randy Faris), **7** (Reuters); ©Getty Images pp. **21** (AFP/ Torsten Blackwood), **18** (DAJ), **20** (Images of Africa), **19** (Photodisc), **4** (Stone); ©iStockphoto p. **29** (Justin Horrocks), ©Science Photo Library pp. **8** (D. Roberts), **15** (Mertyn F. Chillmaid), **6** and **28** (Roger Harris), **12** (Scott Camazine), **16** (Steve Gschmeissner).

Cover photograph of the bones of the shoulder reproduced with permission of ©Getty Images/ 3D4Medical.com.

The publishers would like to thank David Wright for his assistance in the preparation of this book.

Every effort has been made to contact copyright holders of any material reproduced in this book. Any omissions will be rectified in subsequent printings if notice is given to the publishers.

Contents

Any words appearing in the text in bold, **like this**, are explained in the glossary.

What are bones and muscles?

Bones and muscles are the parts of the human body that hold it up and help it move. A car has a metal frame underneath its metal exterior that holds it together. The human machine has a frame of bones beneath the skin. This framework is the **skeleton**. Muscles are attached to the bones. They pull on the bones to move the body.

Looking at bones

The human skeleton is made up of 206 bones. Your bones are on the inside of your body. You cannot see them but you can see their shape, for example when you make a fist or wiggle your toes. Individual bones are hard and rigid, but bones can move at the points where they meet, such as the elbow.

Beneath the metal skin of a car is a complex frame that supports the vehicle throughout its life. This is what the skeleton does for a human body!

It takes more muscles to frown than it does to smile, so smiling should be easier!

Muscles on the move

If a skeleton is the human machine's framework, then muscles are its motors. Muscles produce the forces that move your bones and body around. Without muscles, your skeleton would hold you up but you would be unable to move. There are over 600 muscles in your body. Most actions and movements use many muscles at the same time.

BONES FROM THE PAST

It is because of the hardness of bones that we know about dinosaurs and other animals that lived in the past. When an animal dies, its soft parts rot away. Usually only the hard parts of an animal are preserved as **fossils**. Over millions of years, water that contains **minerals** seeps through the bones. These minerals replace the original bones, creating fossilized bones.

What does the skeleton do?

One of the jobs that the skeleton does is to give the human body its shape. The skeleton is made up of a variety of bones that come in different shapes and sizes.

Sizing up a skeleton

Your different bones help to create your appearance, and define whether you have short fingers, long legs, or a small nose. Your legs are long and straight because the bones inside are long and straight. The **pelvis** is often described as butterfly-shaped. The pelvis connects the **spine** to the leg bones and it helps to give your hips their shape. The ribs are attached to the spine at the back. These 12 pairs of bones curve round to form the shape of your chest at the front.

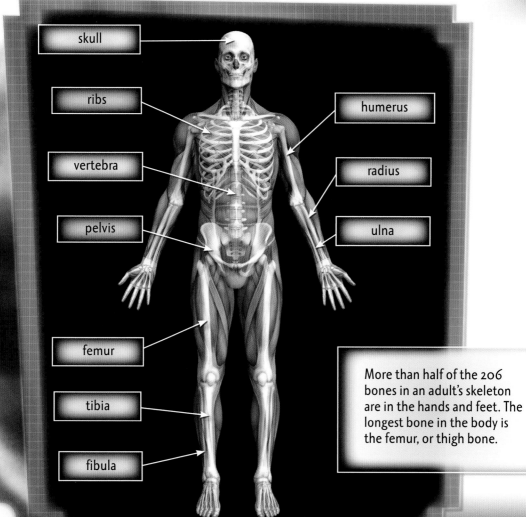

skull

ribs

humerus

vertebra

radius

pelvis

ulna

femur

tibia

fibula

More than half of the 206 bones in an adult's skeleton are in the hands and feet. The longest bone in the body is the femur, or thigh bone.

Skeletons and support

Without a skeleton the human body would be as floppy as a jelly. Your bones support all the other parts of the body. You can think of this as the car's framework carrying the seats inside. For example, the spine, or backbone, holds you upright and supports the other bones of the body when you stand up. The pelvis supports the weight of your upper body when you are sitting down.

Vertebrae are small ring-shaped bones that make up the spine. They are linked together to hold us upright, but the links are flexible enough for us to be able to bend our bodies.

VERTEBRATES AND INVERTEBRATES

Humans and other animals with bony skeletons inside their bodies are called **vertebrates**. Some **invertebrates**, such as snails and insects, have hard shells or tough skins to support the soft body inside. Others, such as earthworms, have bodies tightly filled with liquid to keep their shape.

People protection

A framework doesn't just give a machine its shape and hold it together. It also protects the working parts inside. In a car, those parts include lights and electric wires. In the human machine, the bones of the skeleton protect delicate and sometimes soft body parts.

Different bones or groups of bones protect different body parts. The rib cage protects your heart and lungs. Your heart pumps blood around your body and the lungs help you to breathe. The vertebrae in the spinal column surround the **spinal cord**. This is an important nerve that carries messages between your **brain** and the rest of your body. The skull is a set of bones joined firmly together to form a solid box that keeps your brain safe.

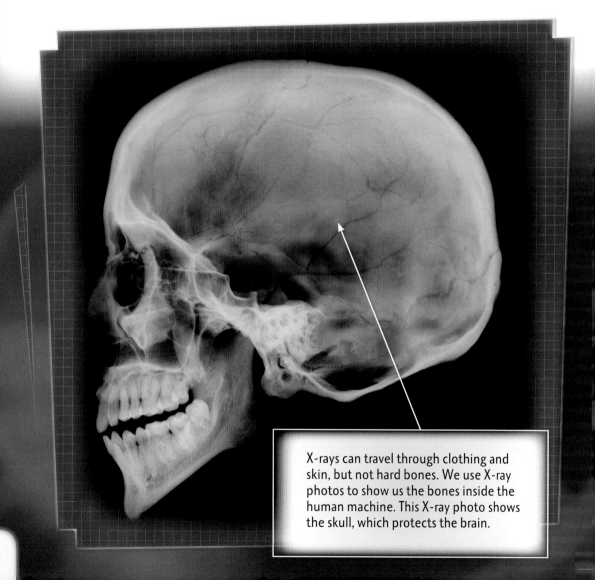

X-rays can travel through clothing and skin, but not hard bones. We use X-ray photos to show us the bones inside the human machine. This X-ray photo shows the skull, which protects the brain.

What are bones made of?

The bones of a skeleton in a museum might look dry and lifeless, but the bones inside you are alive. Each one of us is made up of hundreds of millions of living **cells**. Cells are like tiny building blocks, which grow together to make up the whole body.

Bone cells

Bones are made up of different types of living cells. Some kinds of cells make new bone. Some bone cells carry **nutrients** and waste products to and from **blood vessels** in the bones. Other cells help to shape the bones and help repair damage.

Bones stop growing when people are about 20 years old. At this point your bones are as big as they will ever be. Bone cells keep working though, to repair broken bones and to keep your bones strong and healthy.

At birth a baby has about 300 bones. As children grow, the bones fuse together. An adult has nearly 100 fewer bones than a baby!

Cartilage, calcium, and collagen

Your bones begin to develop before you are born. At first the skeleton is made of **cartilage**. Cartilage is a firm but flexible (bendy) material. Within a few weeks, the process of **ossification** begins. This is when **calcium** and **collagen** replace the cartilage. Calcium is hard and makes bones strong and rigid. Collagen is a bit stretchy, and helps to keep bones a little bit flexible, so they do not snap easily.

Other parts of the body need calcium too. Bones store calcium and release some of it into the blood when it is needed. The blood carries it to other parts of the body.

Drinking milk is a tasty way to keep your calcium levels high.

STRONG BONES

Bones need calcium to make them strong. The body cannot make its own calcium so we have to take it in through the food we eat. Help build healthy bones by eating calcium-rich foods such as milk, cheese, leafy green vegetables, and bony fish.

Looking at bones

Bones have to be strong to support the body's weight without being too heavy for us to move around. Bones contain different amounts of spongy bone and compact bone. Compact bone is **dense**—there are very few spaces or gaps within it. All bones have compact bone on their surface. Compact bone is what makes bones look smooth and solid. Spongy bone is light because it is made up of a mesh, or network, of bones with spaces between them. Spongy bone forms the inside of bones.

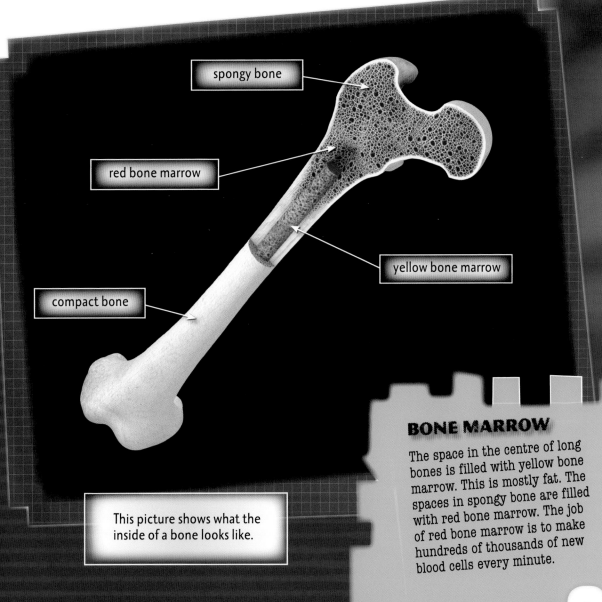

spongy bone

red bone marrow

yellow bone marrow

compact bone

This picture shows what the inside of a bone looks like.

BONE MARROW

The space in the centre of long bones is filled with yellow bone marrow. This is mostly fat. The spaces in spongy bone are filled with red bone marrow. The job of red bone marrow is to make hundreds of thousands of new blood cells every minute.

Different types of bones

There are four main types of bones: long, short, flat, and irregular. Long bones, such as your leg and arm bones, are mostly made of compact bone. Short bones, like the bones in your wrists and ankles, are roughly as long as they are wide. They are mainly made of spongy bone with a thin layer of compact bone on the surface. Flat bones are thin and flat, and are made of a layer of spongy bone between two thin layers of compact bone. Most of the bones of the skull are flat bones. All other bones, including the vertebrae, pelvis and some of the skull bones, are called irregular bones because they have different shapes.

A fracture is a crack or break in a bone. A plaster cast holds the broken pieces together. New bone cells start to grow on either side of the fracture and towards each other until the break is mended.

How do bones fit together?

Bones are connected to other bones at **joints**. Joints are the parts that allow bones to move. At joints, bones are attached to other bones by stretchy straps called **ligaments**.

Ball and socket joints

In ball and socket joints the two bones that meet are different shapes. One bone has a ball-shaped end. This sits inside a cup-shaped area at the end of the other bone (the "socket"). Ball and socket joints are found at your shoulders and hips. They allow movement in every direction.

Hinge joints

Hinge joints act like the hinges on a car door, which allow the door to open and close. They allow a set of bones to move in one direction. Your elbows and knees are hinge joints. These joints allow us to bend and straighten our arms and legs.

When you swing your arms to do the butterfly stroke you are using ball and socket joints in your shoulders!

SPRAINS

If you pull ligaments too far you can sprain them. This happens when the fibres that form ligaments get torn or damaged when they are twisted too hard, so take care when you exercise.

Gliding joints

Gliding joints exist between the surfaces of two flat-ended bones. They only allow a little movement. There are gliding joints in the ankles, wrists, and spine. In the spine there are gliding joints between all 26 vertebrae. Together these joints allow your back to bend and twist.

Immovable joints

Some joints do not move at all. These fixed or immovable joints are found in your skull. The pieces of bone that form a skull fit together like pieces of a jigsaw puzzle. In a baby, there are spaces between the bones in the skull. As a child grows, the spaces between the bones close up.

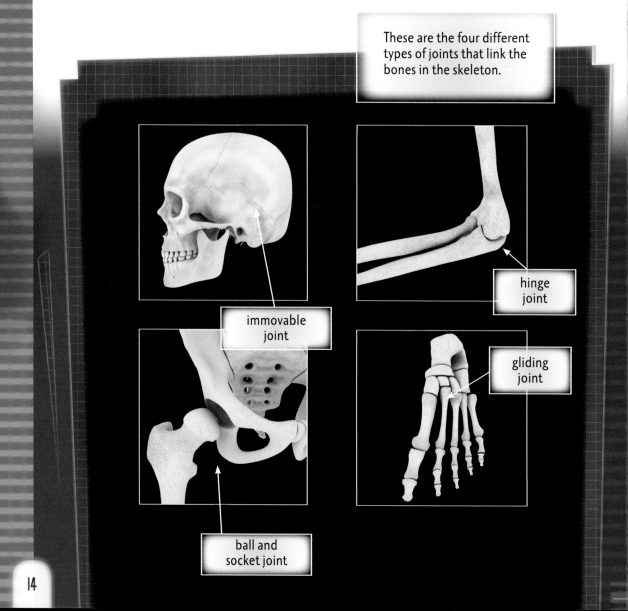

These are the four different types of joints that link the bones in the skeleton.

immovable joint

hinge joint

gliding joint

ball and socket joint

Oiling a machine

Friction is a problem for all machines. When moving parts rub against each other they can wear away. People add oil to machine parts so that the parts slide on the layer of oil rather than rub together. In a human machine, the ends of bones are covered with a thin layer of very smooth cartilage to reduce friction. The joints are also filled with a layer of **synovial fluid**. This oily substance helps bones move more easily. And just like oil in a machine, it also stops bones squeaking as they rub together!

Oil reduces friction between moving parts of a bicycle, just as cartilage and synovial fluid do in a human machine.

DOUBLE JOINTED

Many people can bend a finger or arm in an unusual way. These people are sometimes said to be double jointed, but they do not have twice the usual number of joints. They simply have extra stretchy ligaments that allow their joints to bend more than is normal.

What muscles do we have?

There are three main types of muscle in the body: skeletal, smooth, and cardiac. Skeletal muscles are the muscles that cover the bones of the skeleton.

Skeletal muscles

Skeletal muscles pull the bones and joints only in one direction and yet they are responsible for almost all the movements in the body, from running to smiling. Skeletal muscles are **voluntary** muscles because we control what they do. Your arm muscles only make your arm bend to throw a ball when you want them to. There is a variety of different sizes and shapes of skeletal muscle to allow them to do different jobs.

Thousands of muscle fibres make up each and every skeletal muscle.

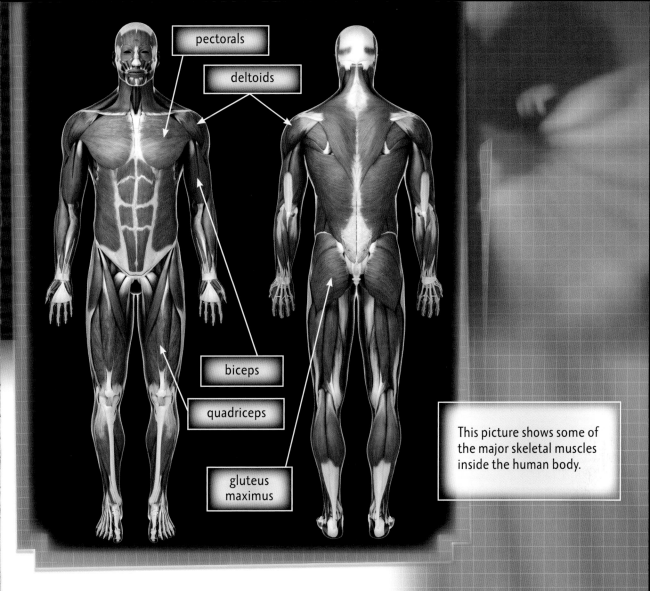

pectorals

deltoids

biceps

quadriceps

gluteus maximus

This picture shows some of the major skeletal muscles inside the human body.

Major skeletal muscles

The chest has large fan-shaped pectoral muscles. These help to pull the arm and shoulder forward. Deltoid muscles are the triangular muscles that help you to move the shoulder and upper arm. Biceps and quadriceps help you move your arms and legs. The largest and strongest skeletal muscles of all are the gluteus maximus, the muscles of the buttocks. These give you the lift you need to jump into the air, sprint off starting blocks, or climb a hill.

STRIPED MUSCLES

Skeletal muscle is also known as striated muscle. "Striated" is another word for "striped". Skeletal muscles are formed from cells which link together to form fibres. They look striped because of the way the fibres are arranged. The fibres are long and thin like rods, crossed with a regular pattern of fine red and white lines. Other muscles in the body are called smooth muscles because they do not have these stripes.

Smooth muscles

Unlike skeletal muscles, which can only work in one direction, smooth muscles can work in all directions. Smooth muscles are found in the walls of certain **organs** of the body, such as the stomach. They are also found in the pipes and tubes inside your body, such as the blood vessels.

Most smooth muscles work automatically without you controlling them. They help to move substances such as blood and food through or around the body. Smooth muscles in your stomach walls squeeze the stomach to help it break down the food inside, so you can digest it. In the walls of the blood vessels, smooth muscles help to squeeze the stream of blood passing through the tubes to keep the flow of blood regular.

The smooth muscles in blood vessels like these help to keep blood flowing in between heart beats.

Cardiac muscle

Cardiac muscle is a kind of striated muscle that is found only in the heart. Unlike skeletal muscle, cardiac muscle works automatically and never gets tired. It makes up most of the heart and it is different from all of the other muscles in the body. It squeezes the chambers of the heart, pumping out blood so it can travel around the body.

Cardiac muscles work all the time, to keep your heart beating even while you are asleep.

EYE MUSCLES

The blue, green or brown coloured part in the middle of the eye is the iris. It contains a ring of smooth muscle. This contracts (squeezes) the iris and changes the size of the pupil, or hole. The pupil changes size to control the light getting into your eye so you can see well.

How do muscles work?

Muscles are like the human machine's engine. They make it move and work. To make a car engine work, you put fuel in its tank. Muscles get the **energy** they need to work from a different kind of fuel—food.

Body fuel

Muscle fuel is **glucose**, a type of sugar. The body obtains glucose from **carbohydrate** foods including pasta, bread, and potatoes. When these foods pass through body parts such as your stomach, they are broken down into tiny particles, or pieces. Some of these particles are glucose, which enter the blood. Blood carries glucose to all of the cells in the body. When muscle fibres need energy, they use this glucose as fuel.

Try to include protein in two of your main meals every day.

MUSCLE-FRIENDLY FOODS

Your muscles also need protein. **Protein** helps the body build healthy muscles and replaces or repairs muscle fibres when they are damaged or get worn out. Proteins are found in foods such as meat, fish, eggs, beans, and nuts.

After extreme exercise, your muscles may run out of energy and your legs may feel wobbly!

Releasing energy

Like other engines, muscles also need **oxygen**. Oxygen is a gas in the air. Car engines need air to burn fuel to release the fuel's energy. In muscle cells glucose and oxygen are used together to release energy. When you breathe you take air into your lungs. This air contains oxygen, which passes from your lungs into the blood. When the heart pumps blood around your body it carries both oxygen and **nutrients** to the cells.

Speeding up

Have you noticed that when you exercise, you breathe harder and your heart beats faster? To produce the energy you need for exercise, your muscles use up the glucose and oxygen in the blood. You breathe harder to get more oxygen and your heart beats faster to pump more blood to the working muscles.

How do muscles move bones?

Skeletal muscles are attached to bones. They pull on the bones to make them move. Muscles cannot push. They can only pull. That is why they work in pairs.

Contracting and relaxing

When a muscle pulls, it **contracts**. The muscle gets tighter, shorter, and harder. If you bend your arm you should be able to feel the muscle on the upper side become firmer as it contracts. When a muscle relaxes it stops pulling and gets longer and softer again.

Muscles in the human machine allow us to lift our arms and move our legs, just as this digger raises and lowers its working arm.

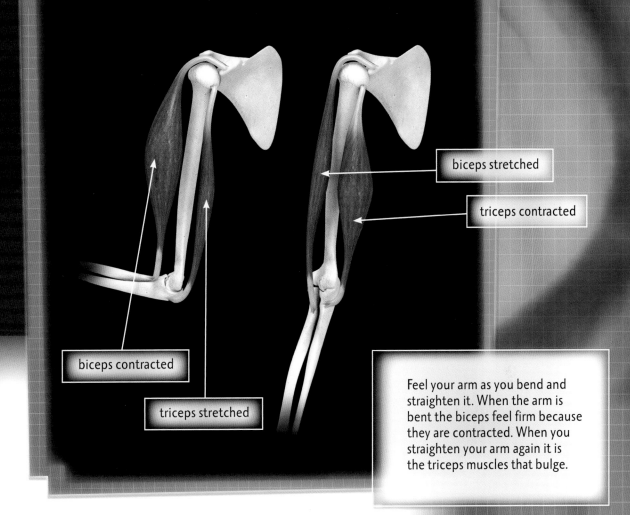

biceps stretched

triceps contracted

biceps contracted

triceps stretched

Feel your arm as you bend and straighten it. When the arm is bent the biceps feel firm because they are contracted. When you straighten your arm again it is the triceps muscles that bulge.

Working together

To make bones move up and down or backwards and forwards, muscles have to work in pairs. Each of the muscles in a pair pulls in a different direction. For example, above the elbow are the triceps and the biceps muscles.

To bend your arm the biceps, the muscle on the upper side of your arm, contracts. This bends the arm at the elbow joint. It also stretches the triceps, the muscle on the lower side of your arm. To lower your arm, it is the turn of the triceps to contract. This straightens the arm again and stretches the biceps muscle instead.

MUSCLE STRAIN

You can tear muscle fibres if you contract or pull muscles too quickly or too hard. This is called muscle strain. You can prevent muscle strain by warming up before sport. A bit of gentle exercise prepares the muscles for activity. It also increases the blood supply to the muscles to give them more energy.

Tendons

Muscles are not directly attached to bones. Muscles are linked to the bones by **tissues** called **tendons**. Tendons are like thick cords. They get tighter when a muscle contracts. When the muscles pull on the tendons, the tendons pull on the bones to make them move. Tendons are vital for large and small movements, from jumping and jogging to wiggling your toes.

Your fingers are operated by muscles in your lower arm. The muscles are attached to the finger bones by tendons that pass through the wrist.

ACHILLES TENDON

The Achilles tendon is the largest tendon in the human body and the easiest to see in action. It is at the back of the ankle and connects the calf muscles to the heel bone. When the calf muscles contract, the Achilles tendon stretches tight and pulls the heel bone up so we can stand on tiptoe!

Controlling muscles

Skeletal muscles are voluntary. They only move when we want them to. The brain is the body's control centre and it tells the skeletal muscles when to move. Messages from the brain travel to the other parts of the body along **nerves**.

Nerves are like telephone wires inside the human machine. Messages, called nerve impulses, travel from the brain, down the spinal cord, and along a system of nerves to the muscles. When a nerve impulse reaches a muscle, it makes the muscle fibres contract.

brain

spinal cord

nerve impulses make the muscles of the leg contract so the leg moves

When you want to move your leg, your brain sends a message down the spinal cord and into nerves in your leg to tell the leg muscles when to contract.

nerves

How can exercise help us?

Exercise is vital for healthy muscles. Exercise makes muscles stronger and bigger because it makes the muscle fibres thicker. Strong muscles work more efficiently and have more **stamina**. They can keep working for longer and are less likely to get injured. Different activities exercise different muscles. Cycling builds strong leg muscles and rowing exercises arm muscles.

Bone care

Your skeleton grows stronger if you do weight-bearing exercise. This means any kind of activity where you support your body's weight, such as tennis, jogging, walking, or dancing. It is vital to exercise to build strong bones when you are young because it is during this time that your bones are growing. Exercise is also good for the joints. It stops them from getting stiff and keeps them moving well.

Aim to exercise at least three times a week for about thirty minutes at a time, or more if you feel like it.

A car has bumpers to protect it from knocks. Protective gear like this can prevent the human machine from being injured when we excercise.

Warm-ups and cool-downs

Warm-ups are gentle exercises that get your muscles ready for sport. Cool-downs help muscles relax again after sport. Warm-up and cool-down exercises can include brisk walking or slow jogging. Or you could gently stretch different parts of the body to loosen up the muscles. As a final warm-up do something a bit more energetic, such as a fast run, to get yourself ready to go. Gentle exercises like these also help to prevent sprains and strains.

PLAY SAFE

Protect your bones and your muscles by wearing the right gear for different kinds of exercise. For example, wear running shoes with grip so you don't slip, and wear a helmet for cycling. For some activities, such as skateboarding, you should wear knee, wrist, and elbow pads as well as a helmet.

The world's most complex machine

The human body is often described as the world's most complex machine, but of course it is not really a machine at all. Machines are non-living, mechanical objects, whereas our bodies are natural, living things. But there are similarities. Like a machine, the body is made up of different parts that work together in systems to do particular jobs. These different systems work together to make the whole body – or the human machine – run smoothly and efficiently.

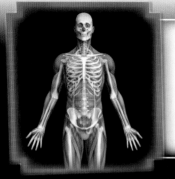

THE SKELETAL SYSTEM

This system of bones supports the other parts of the body, rather as the metal frame of a car supports the vehicle.

THE DIGESTIVE SYSTEM

The digestive system works as a food-processing machine. It consists of various organs that work together to break down food into forms that the body can use as fuel and raw materials.

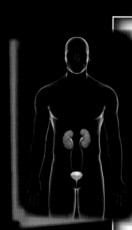

THE EXCRETORY SYSTEM

This is the human machine's waste disposal system, removing harmful substances and waste produced by the other parts of the body.

THE NERVOUS SYSTEM

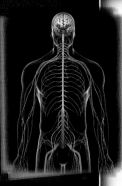

This is the human machine's communication and control system. The brain transmits and receives messages from the senses and the rest of the body. It does this through a network of nerves connected to the brain via the spinal cord.

THE CIRCULATORY SYSTEM

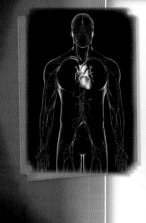

This is the body's delivery system. The heart pumps blood through blood vessels, carrying nutrients and oxygen to the other parts and removing waste from cells.

THE RESPIRATORY SYSTEM

This system provides the rest of the body with the oxygen it needs to get energy from food. It also releases waste gases from the body into the air.

THE MUSCULAR SYSTEM

Muscles are the human machine's motors. Some muscles make the bones of the skeleton move; others work as pumps to keep substances moving through the body.

Glossary

blood vessel hollow tube that carries blood in the body

brain organ in the head that controls all the body's activities

calcium mineral that gives bones their strength

carbohydrate kind of food, such as pasta, that gives us energy

cartilage softer and more rubbery substance than bone, usually found between bones

cells building block or basic unit of all living things

collagen substance found in the bones, cartilage, and tendons that is strong but slightly stretchy

contract when a muscle contracts, it tightens. This causes it to pull on a bone if it is attached to one.

dense tightly packed together

energy the ability to move, grow, or do anything that living things do

fossil remains of a plant or animal that lived long ago

friction force that causes resistance when two surfaces or objects rub against each other

glucose kind of sugar that the body obtains from carbohydrate foods

invertebrate animal that doesn't have a bony skeleton inside its body

joint place where two bones meet

ligament band of fibres that connects bones across joints

mineral non-living substance, such as salt, sand, or calcium

nerve bundle of fibres that carries messages between the brain and the rest of the body

nutrient substance that plants and animals need to grow and survive

organ part of the body that performs a specific function

ossification process by which soft cartilage hardens into bone

oxygen gas in the air

pelvis bone that forms the hips and to which the legs are attached

skeleton network of bones that provides a frame for the human body

spinal cord bundle of nerves inside the spine, which runs from the brain down the length of the back

spine column of individual bones called vertebrae that link to form the backbone

stamina someone with stamina does not get worn our easily

synovial fluid slippery, oil-like substance that lubricates joints

tendon tough, cord-like fibres that attach muscles to bones

tissue group of cells of the same sort that do a job together

vertebrae column of individual bones (vertebra) that make up the spine or backbone

vertebrate animal that has a bony skeleton inside its body

voluntary to do something by choice after thinking about it

Find out more

Websites

At www.bbc.co.uk/science/humanbody/ there is an interactive information section in which you can build a skeleton, stretch some muscles, and organize the organs in a human body.

At www.kidshealth.org/kid/body/bones_SW.html you will find "The Big Story on Bones" and the kidshealth website also has useful sections on muscles and other human body topics.

At http://insideout.rigb.org/insideout/anatomy/tissue_issues/muscles.html there is information about muscles and links to other human body topics and also interactive games to play such as "Pump some Iron" and answers to some fascinating questions such as "Can engineers learn from the human body?"

At www.cartage.org.lb/en/kids/science/Biology%20Cells/Muscle/mainpage.htm you can find lots more details about individual muscles and how muscles work.

Books

Body: An Amazing Tour of Human Anatomy, Robert Winston (Dorling Kindersley, 2005)

Exploring the Human Body: The Skeleton and Muscles, Carol Ballard (Franklin Watts, 2005)

Movers and Shapers: Bones, Muscles and Joints, Patricia Macnair (Kingfisher Books, 2004)

The Skeleton and Muscles, Steve Parker (Hodder Wayland, 2006)

Index